Remember the good times.

You are my beary best friend in the whole world.

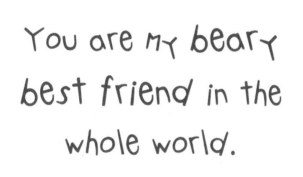

"The only way to have
a friend is to be one."

-Ralph Waldo Emerson

Those you rely on are the friends whose hearts beat in rhythm to yours.

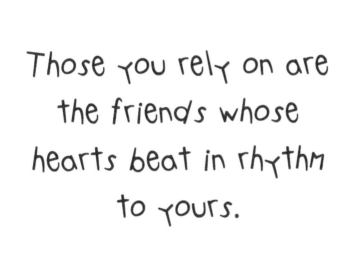

"Yes, we must ever be friends; and of all who offer you friendship . . .

Let me be the first,
the truest, the nearest
and dearest."

-Henry Wadsworth Longfellow

On the days you need
a friend the most,
don't be surprised to
find her on your
doorstep.

You listen to the ups
and downs of my life
just when I need it
most.

"Friendship is the only cement that will hold the world together."

-Anonymous

We turn to our
friends with our most
precious dreams.

Our path of friendship has been a journey of fun, excitement, and bear necessities.

"Friendship redoubleth joys and cutteth griefs in half."

-Francis Bacon

Share a dream with a friend and what happens? Suddenly, you have all the encouragement you need.

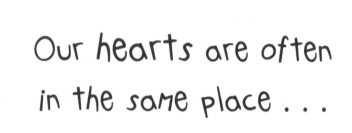

Our hearts are often
in the same place . . .

Even when our spirits
are far apart.

"'Stay' is a charming word in a friend's vocabulary."

-Louisa May Alcott

No matter what you
said to each other,
there are no winners.
Take a deep breath
and pick up the phone.

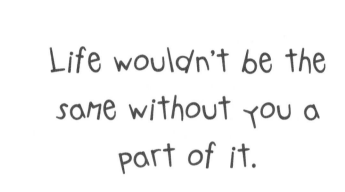

Life wouldn't be the same without you a part of it.

When I find myself
fading, I close my
eyes and realize my
friends are my
energy."

-Anonymous

You are who you are
and I'm happy to say
that who you are
makes me beary
happy.

"The road to a
friend's house is
never long."

-Danish Proverb

Friends know how to find the best and worst in each other and are honest enough to live with both.

Our hearts
understand each
other. Our lives weave
in and out of the
passage of time.

"A friend is a gift
you give yourself."

-Robert Louis Stevenson

Do you really think
you could make it
through your next
worst day without
your girlfriend?

The reasons we are friends? How much time do you have?

"The better part of
one's life consists of
friendships."

-Abraham Lincoln

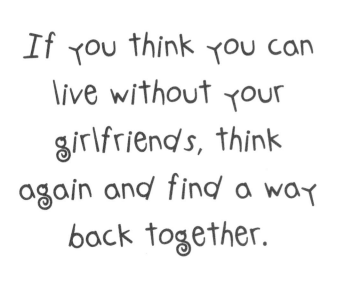

If you think you can live without your girlfriends, think again and find a way back together.

Count the times you
were glad to have a
friend. Now send your
friend beary happy
wishes.

"Some people go to priests; others to poetry; I to my friends."

-Virginia Woolf

The passage of our
common lives stitched
together over time
forms a quilt of new
journeys.

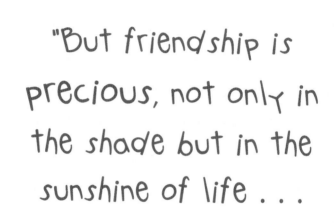

"But friendship is precious, not only in the shade but in the sunshine of life . . .

And thanks to a
benevolent
arrangement of things,
the greater part of
life is sunshine."

-Thomas Jefferson

Thank you for all the
times I counted on
you to be there and
you were.

My dream for you is
to find happiness
always.

There are friends,
and then there's an
incredible friend
like you.

In the silence
between our times
together, our roots
grow deep.

Bear hugs for my
friend who deserves
the best of all things.

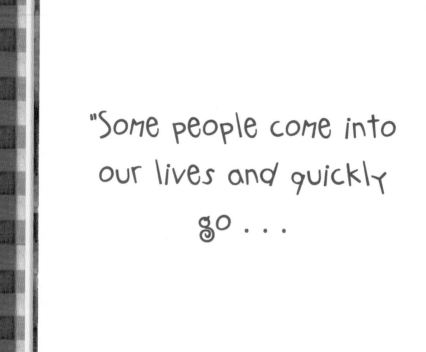

"Some people come into our lives and quickly go . . .

Others stay awhile,
make footprints on
our hearts, and we
are never, ever the
same."

-Unknown

A cup of coffee with
a girlfriend starts the
day off right.

The comfort of an old friend is nourishment to the soul.

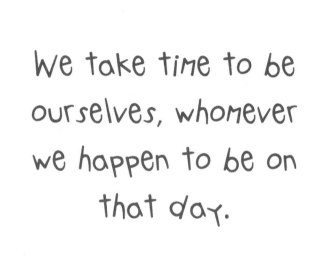

We take time to be ourselves, whomever we happen to be on that day.

"Friendship is
certainly the finest
balm for the pangs of
disappointed love."

-Unknown

"Love is like the wild rose-briar; friendship is like the holly tree . . .

The holly is dark when
the rose-briar blooms.
But which will bloom
more constantly?"

-Emily Bronte

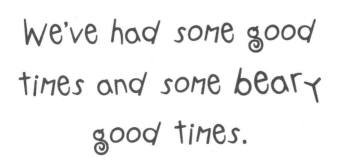

We've had some good times and some beary good times.

"Love is blind.
Friendship closes its
eyes."

-Anonymous

We share our time and our voices to make the world a better place.

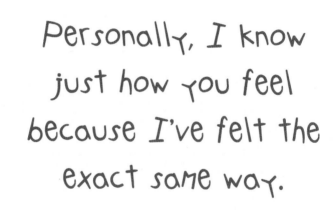

Personally, I know just how you feel because I've felt the exact same way.

We don't think about
someday. We plan our
fun for today.

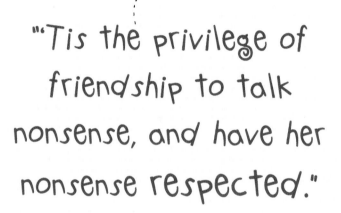

"'Tis the privilege of friendship to talk nonsense, and have her nonsense respected."

-Charles Lamb

You make me laugh,
even when I think I'm
in a bad mood.

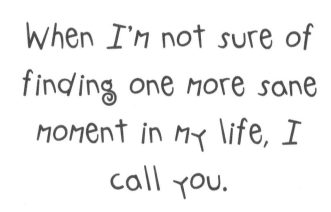

When I'm not sure of finding one more sane moment in my life, I call you.

A friend like you
makes the world go
round.

"The most I can do
for my friend is simply
be a friend."

-Henry David Thoreau

You've been beary
kind to me.
Thank you, friend.

© 2004 Havoc Publishing
San Diego, California
U.S.A.

Text by Maureen Webster

ISBN 0-7416-4113-5

www.havocpub.com

Made in China